Yeshua Revealed

In the

Feasts of Israel

Dr. Rick Kurnow

ISBN-13:
978-1496113788

ISBN-10:
1496113780

Dedication

To : Yeshua (Jesus) The Living Word,
The Light of the World. The Precious Lamb of God.

Introduction

Learning about the Feasts of Israel reveals a beautiful picture of symbolism that points to Yeshua (Jesus) the Messiah. God's plan from the beginning was to send His Son into this world to redeem all people from the penalty, power and presence of sin. It is interesting to note that Jesus died on Passover when the sacrificial lamb was slain. Jesus is referred to as the Lamb of God.

John 1:29
"Behold! The Lamb of God who takes away the sin of the world! "

Then He rose from the dead on the Feast of the First fruits which in Hebrew is called bikkurim. He rose from the dead the same hour the sheaf was presented as a wave offering of the first fruits of the barley harvest. It was then the counting of the omer started for 50 days.

1Corinthians 15:20-23
"But now is Christ risen from the dead, and become the first fruits of them that slept. For since by man came death, by man came also the resurrection of the dead. For as in Adam all die, even so in Christ shall all be made alive. But every man in his own order: Christ the firstfruits; afterward they that are Christ's at His Coming"

50 days from Passover He sent His Holy Spirit on the Feast of Pentecost which in Hebrew is called Shavuot. The celebration of Shavuot is the celebration of the giving of the law through Moses.

In the following chapters we are going to learn about the meaning of these feasts, how they are celebrated and how they all point to Yeshua. If you are Jewish and you are reading this book , I pray that your eyes will be opened to see Yeshua as the Messiah. If you are a believer in Yeshua already, I pray that your life and walk with the Lord will be strengthened as you discover the amazing revelations hidden in the feasts of Israel ready for you to discover. The more you see, the more you will see Yeshua.

I love the tapestry that God has woven over time. When you look at this tapestry on display for all to see, you will see the most beautiful picture of the Messiah Yeshua. As you inspect this tapestry closer you will discover details that you never knew existed. Get ready for wonderful truths that paint this picture of the Messiah for all people, Yeshua Ha Mashiach (Jesus the Messiah).

I want to encourage you to learn more about the Biblical feasts of Israel. The more you learn the more you will discover God's wonderful plan of redemption and His covenant promises that He has made to you and me.

Table of Contents

All scripture quotations are from the New King James Version unless otherwise noted

Chapter 1

The Feasts Point to Yeshua (Jesus)

John 5:39

"You search the Scriptures, for in them you think you have eternal life; and these are they which testify of Me".

Search the scriptures and you will discover a rich tapestry of woven through time by God, a tapestry that reveals Yeshua the Messiah. Every thread of scripture points to Him. Study the Tabernacle of Moses and you will see that everything in the tabernacle points to Him.

The Feasts of Israel were very important to Yeshua when He walked on this earth. He celebrated them. He embraced them and He gave prophetic meaning and revelation of the message of each feast.

The Times and Seasons of the Feasts

Leviticus 23:4

"These are the feasts of the LORD, holy convocations which you shall proclaim at their appointed times."

God gave Moses instructions concerning the feasts. The entire chapter of Leviticus 23 reveals the appointed times and seasons. It was on Mt. Sinai that God gave Moses specific instructions concerning seven feasts.

1. Passover (Pesach) Nisan 14-22
2. Unleavened Bread (Chag Hamotzi) – Nisan 15-22
3. First Fruits (Yom Habikkurim) – Nisan 16
4. Pentecost (Shavu'ot) – Sivan 6-7
5. Trumpets (Rosh Hashanah) - Tishri 1
6. Atonement (Yom Kippur) – Tishri 10
7. Tabernacles (Sukkot) – Tishri 15-22

The feasts are based on the Jewish calendar which is based on the phases of the moon. Each month in the lunar calendar begins with a new moon. The Gregorian calendar which has January through December is a solar based calendar based on 365 days a year. The feasts of Israel always happen on the same days each year but because the lunar calendar is different from the solar calendar the feasts fall on different days on the Gregorian calendar.

There are the spring feasts and the fall feasts. Three of the feasts occur near the beginning of spring, one in late spring and then three in fall. There are two other feasts celebrated that are not listed in Leviticus 23. One is the Feast of Purim based on the book of Esther and the other was prophesied in Daniel 8:9-14, The Feast of Dedication known as Chanukah. This feast was started after the fulfillment of the prophecy.

Jewish Month	Gregorian Calendar Date	Feast Celebrated during these Months
Nissan	March–April	Passover
Iyar	April–May	
Sivan	May–June	Shavuot
Tammuz	June–July	
Menachem Av	July–August	Tisha B'Av
Elul	August–September	
Tishrei	September–October	Rosh Hashanah ,Yom Kippur, Sukkot
Marcheshvan	October–November	
Kislev	November–December	Chanukah
Tevet	December–January	Conclusion of Chanukah
Shevat	January–February	
Adar	February–March	Purim

Chapter 2

The Last Supper

Passover

Passover pronounced in Hebrew "Pesach" is one of my favorite feasts when it comes to discovering Yeshua and the covenant that God has made with His people. The feast starts on Nisan 14 and moves right into the Feast of Unleavened Bread. On the third day of Passover the Feast of First Fruits is celebrated and the counting of the omer begins for 50 days.

The crucifixion happened the same hour the paschal lamb was sacrificed and the resurrection took place at the same hour the sheaf was waved as the first fruits of the barley harvest. Yeshua rose from the dead on the celebration of "Bikkurim" first fruits. The resurrection of Yeshua is the New Testament fulfillment of the Feast of First fruits.

The seder meal that is celebrated on Passover points to Yeshua. In fact the "Last Supper" that Yeshua had with His disciples was a seder meal celebrating the Passover. There are many aspects of the seder meal that many Christians do not know about, but Yeshua gave rich meaning to these things. Discovering these truths will enrich your relationship with Him and will open your eyes to the covenant God has made with you.

Matthew 26:17-19
Now on the first day of the Feast of the Unleavened Bread the disciples came to Jesus, saying to Him, "Where do You want us to prepare for You to eat the Passover?"18 And He said, "Go into the city to a certain man, and say to him, 'The Teacher says, "My time is at hand; I will keep the Passover at your house with My disciples."19 So the disciples did as Jesus had directed them; and they prepared the Passover.

When the Jewish people prepare for the Passover seder meal they go through their house and remove all leaven from their homes before they can hold the feast. Also they do not eat anything that has leaven in for the full seven days of the feast.

Exodus 12:15a
"Seven days you shall eat unleavened bread. On the first day you shall remove leaven from your houses..."

This practice shows us a principle that we can apply to our spiritual lives. Paul the Apostle who was a Jewish believer in Yeshua, celebrated the Feast of Passover all his life. He was very familiar with this practice. In his writing to the Corinthian people, he used this practice to illustrate some spiritual truths.

14

1 Corinthians 5:6-8

"Your glorying is not good. Do you not know that a little leaven leavens the whole lump? Therefore purge out the old leaven, that you may be a new lump, since you truly are unleavened. For indeed Christ, our Passover, was sacrificed for us. Therefore let us keep the feast, not with old leaven, nor with the leaven of malice and wickedness, but with the unleavened bread of sincerity and truth."

Preparing the seder meal has certain elements that carry symbolism to tell the story of God's deliverance of the Children of Israel from Egypt. These different items are represented on the seder plate..

Zeroah: A Roasted shank bone of a lamb
This reminds us of sacrificed lamp whose blood was put on the doorposts. The Hebrew word for bone is "etzem" but the term "zero'a" is used which means arm – as in "outstretched arm"

Beitzah: A roasted hard-boiled Egg
This reminds us of the roasted slaughtered lamb that was brought to the Holy Temple on Pesach as a sacrifice for sins.

Maror: Horseradish Root
These bitter herbs symbolize the harsh suffering and bitter times the children of Israel suffered when they were slaves in Egypt.

Charoset: A sweet mixture of chopped fruit, nuts and seasonings. Ground up together, Charoset resembles bricks and mortar, reminding us how hard the children of Israel were forced to work when they were slaves in Egypt.

Karpas: This can be a small slice of onion, boiled potato or sprigs of parsley. We dip the Karpas into salt water at the beginning of the Seder, representing the salty tears the children of Israel cried when they were slaves.

Chazeret: Romaine Lettuce
This is the second portion of bitter herbs which we eat during the Seder.

The Breaking of The Matzah (Unleavened Bread)

During the Seder the unleavened bread is taken from a three compartment cloth pouch called a Matzah Tosh. The word "tosh" means "unity". The matzah is taken from the center compartment and broken in half. It was at this point in the seder that Yeshua took the middle piece and broke it. It is interesting to note that the three compartment Matzah Tosh can symbolize the Trinity. The Father, Son and Holy Spirit. When Jewish people are asked about the three compartments of the Matzah Tosh they have differing opinions. Some say it represents the patriarchs, Abraham, Isaac & Jacob. There are several other opinions. But I say that it represents the unity of the Godhead. Yeshua specifically took the center piece and declared it was His body.

Luke 22:19
And He took bread, gave thanks and broke it, and gave it to them, saying, "This is My body which is given for you; do this in remembrance of Me."

This prophetic act spoke of covenant. We are reminded of the covenant that God made with Abraham. When God established His covenant with Abraham He told Abram to take animals and cut them in two and place them side to side. Then God passed between the pieces of flesh establishing a covenant with him.

Genesis 15:10

Then he brought all these to Him and cut them in two, down the middle, and placed each piece opposite the other

Genesis 15:17-18

And it came to pass, when the sun went down and it was dark, that behold, there appeared a smoking oven and a burning torch that passed between those pieces. On the same day the LORD made a covenant with Abram

The act of walking between the pieces of flesh was an act of covenant in ancient biblical times. It was called "The walk of death". The person initiating the covenant would pass through the pieces of flesh and declare "Let it be done to me as it has been done to these animals if I do not keep the word of this agreement"

When Yeshua died on the cross the veil of the Temple was torn from top to bottom. This spoke of covenant. It spoke of His body broken for us. This veil represented the flesh of Yeshua.

Hebrews 10:19-21

Therefore, brethren, having boldness to enter the Holiest by the blood of Jesus, 20 by a new and living way which He consecrated for us, through the veil, that is, His flesh,

The first thing Yeshua did when He died on the cross was walk between the pieces of flesh and establish the New Covenant.

Hebrews 9:11-15

But Christ came as High Priest of the good things to come, with the greater and more perfect tabernacle not made with hands, that is, not of this creation.12 Not with the blood of goats and calves, but **with His own blood He entered the Most Holy Place** *once for all, having obtained eternal redemption.13 For if the blood of bulls and goats and the ashes of a heifer, sprinkling the unclean, sanctifies for the purifying of the flesh,14 how much more shall the blood of Christ, who through the eternal Spirit offered Himself without spot to God, cleanse your conscience from dead works to serve the living God?15 And for this reason* **He is the Mediator of the new covenant**, *by means of death, for the redemption of the transgressions under the first covenant, that those who are called may receive the promise of the eternal inheritance.*

The Hebrew word for covenant is "karath beriyth" which means to make an agreement by the cutting of flesh and the shedding of blood. Yeshua was setting the stage for the New Covenant when He took the middle piece of the matzah and broke it in two making the declaration that it represented His body broken for you and me and when the veil of the temple was torn from top to bottom.

The Afikomen

What is the "Afikomen" ? After the Matzah is broken in two one piece is wrapped in a cloth or napkin and then hidden away to be discovered later. This is called the

Afikomen. At the end of the seder meal the children search for the afikomen and the one who discovers it is rewarded with a gift. The word "Afikomen" was adopted into the Hebrew language from the Greek language. The word actually means in Greek "He came" If you ask many Jewish people today about this word they do not know the true history and meaning of this word. Think about it. Yeshua was crucified. Wrapped in grave cloths and hidden in a tomb. Now those who discovered that He came are rewarded with salvation.

The Dipping of the Sweet & the Bitter Together

The other piece of matzah is taken dipped in the seder plate putting together two of the elements on the seder plate, the Maror which is the bitter herb and the Charoseth, which is the sweet mixture are put together while telling the story of the slavery the children of Israel endured while slaves in Egypt. The Charoseth represented the mortar used to build the pyramids in Egypt. The Maror represented the bitterness and harshness of their labors and slavery in Egypt. The matzah is taken and is dipped into the dish with the bitter and the sweet and put together and eaten. What this represents to the Jewish people is that the labors and slavery were harsh and difficult but they had a hope that a deliver would come. So the sweetness represented that hope and made their labors easier to endure.

Yeshua knew that He was about to enter into the most difficult time of His life and it started with a betrayal of one of the closest to him. Judas who walked and served with Him for three years was about to betray Yeshua and He knew this. He used the dipping of the bitter and the sweet together to reveal this betrayal and to send the message of hope that He was the deliverer sent to deliver all people from the slavery of sin.

Mark 14:18-20
Now as they sat and ate, Jesus said, "Assuredly, I say to you, one of you who eats with Me will betray Me." And they began to be sorrowful, and to say to Him one by one, "Is it I?" And another said, "Is it I?" He answered and said to them, "It is one of the twelve, who dips with Me in the dish.

Hebrews 12:2
"Looking unto Jesus, the author and finisher of our faith, who for the joy that was set before Him endured the cross, despising the shame, and has sat down at the right hand of the throne of God."

When Yeshua dipped the Matzah with Judas in the dish He knew His betrayal was going to be bitter and what He was about to go through was going to be very painful. But He had a hope, and it was you and Me. Knowing He would redeem all mankind gave Him the joy He needed to take Him through all He was about to endure.

The Four Cups

There are four cups during the seder meal that the people drink. Each cup is based on Exodus 6:6,7 and have very specific meanings.

Exodus 6:6-7
Therefore say to the children of Israel: 'I am the LORD; I will bring you out from under the burdens of the Egyptians, I will rescue you from their bondage, and I will redeem you with an outstretched arm and with great judgments. I will

take you as My people, and I will be your God. Then you shall know that I am the LORD your God who brings you out from under the burdens of the Egyptians.

The First Cup – The Cup of Sanctification

Exodus 6:6a

"I will bring you out from under the burdens of the Egyptians"

The Second Cup – The Cup of Judgment

Exodus 6:6b

"I will rescue you from their bondage"

The Third Cup- The Cup of Redemption

Exodus 6:6c

"I will redeem you with an outstretched arm and with great judgments."

The Fourth Cup- The Cup of Completion

Exodus 6:7

I will take you as My people, and I will be your God.

The first two cups of the seder meal are drank before the meal. The first cup of sanctification speaks of God taking His people out of bondage and setting them apart as holy unto Him.

1 Peter 2:9-10
9 But you are a chosen generation, a royal priesthood, a holy nation, His own special people, that you may proclaim the praises of Him who called you out of darkness into His marvelous light;10 who once were not a people but are now the people of God, who had not obtained mercy but now have obtained mercy.

The second cup of judgment shows that God will judge our enemies and rescue us from their bondage.

John 16:11
Of judgment, because the ruler of this world is judged.

Colossians 2:15
Having disarmed principalities and powers, He made a public spectacle of them, triumphing over them in it.

The two remaining cups carry the most significance and point to Yeshua and what He has accomplished for us. These cups are drank after the meal. The third cup is referred to as the cup of redemption and is based on *"I will redeem you with an outstretched arm and with great judgments."*

Luke 22:20
*Likewise He also took **the cup after supper**, saying, "This cup is the new covenant in My blood, which is shed for you.*

We know that Yeshua outstretched His arms on the cross to redeem us. Yeshua specifically took the cup after the supper which is the Cup of Redemption and He said it represented the New Covenant in His blood. The cup was known to represent the blood of the lamb that was placed on the doorposts of the people's homes to protect them when the death angel passed over.

Exodus 12:13
Now the blood shall be a sign for you on the houses where you are. And when I see the blood, I will pass over you; and the plague shall not be on you to destroy you when I strike the land of Egypt.

We truly are redeemed by the blood of the lamb, The Lamb of God who takes away the sins of the world. His new covenant with us removes and delivers us from the penalty, power and presence of sin.

It is interesting to note that Yeshua did not drink the fourth cup at the seder meal. The fourth cup is based on *"I will take you as My people, and I will be your God."* He could not drink this cup at the supper because He had not yet paid the price for our sins and therefore could not fulfill the fourth cup of taking us as His people and He being our God. He knew that He must drink that cup but He knew what He was about to go through. How do we know He did not drink this cup?

Matthew 26:27-30
Then He took the cup, and gave thanks, and gave it to them, saying, "Drink from it, all of you. For this is My blood of the new covenant, which is shed for many for the remission of sins. But I say to you, I will not drink of this fruit of the vine from now on until that day when I drink it new with you in My Father's kingdom."

This scripture clearly shows that after He drank the Cup of Redemption declaring it to represent the blood of the new covenant, that He would not drink again until He drank it new with us in His Father's kingdom. Many think He is referring to the Marriage Supper of The Lamb in Revelations. I say He is referring to the time when He would be able to fulfill Exodus 6:7 *"I will take you as My people, and I will be your God."* The time when we become one with Him at salvation. Whenever two joined together in marriage they would always complete the covenant with drinking a cup together.

After Yeshua drank the third cup, He sang a song with His disciples and they left and went to the Garden of Gethsemane. What happens and what does He say?

Matthew 26:39
*He went a little farther and fell on His face, and prayed, saying, "O My Father, if it is possible, let **this cup** pass from Me; nevertheless, not as I will, but as You will."*

Matthew 26:42
*Again, a second time, He went away and prayed, saying, "O My Father, if **this cup** cannot pass away from Me unless I drink it, Your will be done."*

John 18:10-11
Then Simon Peter, having a sword, drew it and struck the high priest's servant, and cut off his right ear. The servant's name was Malchus. Then Jesus said to Peter, "Put your

*sword into the sheath. Shall I not drink **the cup** which My Father has given Me?"*

Mark 15:21-24
And they brought Him to the place Golgotha, which is translated, Place of a Skull. Then they gave Him wine mingled with myrrh to drink, but He did not take it.

Throughout His journey to the cross where He was crucified He kept mentioning "the cup". What cup was He referring to? Why did He keep mentioning the cup? He was referring to the cup of completion. He resolved in His heart that He would drink the cup in the Garden of Gethsemane. But He could not drink it yet.

When He finally knew He had completed bearing all the sins of the world on Himself. When He had finally paid the ultimate price for our redemption. Then He declared it was complete and He drank that cup.

John 19:28-30
*After this, Jesus, knowing **that all things were now accomplished, that the Scripture might be fulfilled, said, "I thirst!"** Now a vessel full of sour wine was sitting there; and they filled a sponge with sour wine, put it on hyssop, and put it to His mouth. **So when Jesus had received the sour wine, He said, "It is finished!"** And bowing His head, He gave up His spirit.*

It is finished, it is complete. Yeshua made a way for you and me to become His people and He become our God. When we receive His finished work He comes into our lives by the Holy Spirit (Ruach Ha Kodesh) and establishes His kingdom in us. We then share in communion with Him. We are made whole because His body was broken for us and we drink the cup of completion new with Him in the kingdom of God.

Luke 17:20-21
*Now when He was asked by the Pharisees when the kingdom of God would come, He answered them and said, "The kingdom of God does not come with observation; 21 nor will they say, 'See here!' or 'See there!' For indeed, **the kingdom of God is within you**."*

Wherever the King has dominion
That is where the Kingdom is.

Chapter 3
The Ressurection

The Festival of First Fruits (Bikkurim)

The fifteenth of Nisan begins *Hag HaMatzah* (the Feast of Unleavened Bread), It is a seven day feast to the Lord. The day following the sabbath during Passover is called the Feast of First Fruits (Leviticus 23:9-14).

The feast was celebrated in this way, when the standing ripe harvest of barley and wheat was ready to be reaped. The celebrant would take one sheaf from the standing harvest and bring it to the priest. The lone sheaf was called "the sheaf of the first fruits." The priest was then to take this one sheaf and wave it before the Lord in His house. This was to be done "the day after the sabbath." Other offerings were also to be presented along with the sheaf.

God commanded the people to bring a sheaf of the harvest (Leviticus 23:10). The Hebrew word for "sheaf" is *omer*. An *omer* is defined as "a measure of dry things, containing a tenth part of an ephah." The definition of an *omer* being a tenth part of an ephah is found in Exodus 16:36. An ephah contains 10 *omers* of grain. Remember, three times a year God commanded the people to come to Jerusalem to celebrate the festivals of Passover (*Pesach*), Pentecost (*Shavuot*), and Tabernacles (*Sukkot*). All three of these festivals are agricultural harvest festivals. Passover (*Pesach*) is the barley harvest. Pentecost (*Shavuot*) is the wheat harvest. Both of these festivals are first fruits harvests before the final harvest that was to come at the end of the year during the festival of Tabernacles (*Sukkot*), which is the fruit harvest.

The harvest represents all who would put their faith, trust, and confidence in the Messiah *Yeshua* (Matthew 13:39; Mark 4:26-29; Luke 10:1-12; Revelation 14:14-16). So, the sheaf is the first of the first fruits. Since a sheaf in the Bible is used to typify a person or persons, a sheaf spiritually represents people who accept the Messiah into their hearts.

The nation of Israel was familiar with the concept of first fruits or the firstborn. The first fruits were always the choicest, the foremost, the first, the best, the preeminent of all that was to follow. They were holy to the Lord. The concept of first fruits or firstborn is a major theme in the Bible. This can be seen by the following Scriptures: Exodus 23:16,19: 34:26; Leviticus 2:12,14; 23:20; Numbers 18:12-15,26; Deuteronomy 18:1-5; 26:2-4,10; 2 Chronicles 31:5; Nehemiah 10:35-39; Proverbs 3:9; Jeremiah 2:3; Ezekiel 44:30; 48:14; Malachi 3:8-14; Hebrews 6:20; 7:1-8.

Everything on the earth, both man and beast, was to be presented before the Lord as first fruits to Him.

1. The firstborn of both man and beast were sanctified (made holy) and presented to the Lord (Exodus 13:2; 22:29).
2. The first fruits of all the earth were presented to the L-rd at His altar in praise and thanksgiving (Deuteronomy 26:1-11).

The Seventeenth of Nisan

Resurrection and Salvation

The theme of the festival of First Fruits is resurrection and salvation. There are several important events that happened on this day in the Bible.

1. Noah's ark rests on Mount Ararat (Genesis 8:4).
2. Israel crosses the Red Sea (Exodus 3:18; 5:3, 14).
3. Israel eats the first fruits of the Promised Land (Joshua 5:10-12). The manna that God gave from Heaven during the days in the wilderness ceased the sixteenth day of Nisan after the people ate of the old corn of the land. The day following was the seventeenth of Nisan, the day when the children of Israel ate the first fruits of the Promised Land.
4. The resurrection of *Yeshua*, the Messiah (John 12:24; 1 Corinthians 15:16-20). *Yeshua* celebrated the festival of First Fruits by offering Himself as the first fruits to all future generations (Matthew 27:52-53).

Yeshua Is the First Fruits of the Barley Harvest

1. *Yeshua* is the firstborn of Miryam (Mary) (Matthew 1:23-25).
2. *Yeshua* is the first-begotten of God the Father (Hebrews 1:6).
3. *Yeshua* is the firstborn of every creature (Colossians 1:15).
4. *Yeshua* is the first-begotten from the dead (Revelation 1:5).
5. *Yeshua* is the firstborn of many brethren (Romans 8:29).

6. *Yeshua* is the first fruits of the resurrected ones (1 Corinthians 15:20,23).
7. *Yeshua* is the beginning of the creation of God (Revelation 3:14).
8. *Yeshua* is the preeminent One (Colossians 1:18).

First Fruits Is Prophetic of the Resurrection of the Messiah

The festival of the sheaf of the first fruits is prophetic of the resurrection of *Yeshua*. *Yeshua* prophesied that He would rise three days and nights after He was slain on the tree (Matthew 12:38-40; 16:21; Luke 24:44-46). This was foreshadowed to happen in the *Tanach* (Old Testament) by type and shadow (Genesis 22:1-6; Exodus 3:18; 5:3; 8:27; Esther 4:15-17; Jonah 1:7; 2:1-2).

Since *Yeshua* was slain on the tree on the day of Passover (*Pesach*), the fourteenth of Nisan, and He arose from the grave three days and nights after He was slain, *Yeshua* arose from the grave on the seventeenth of Nisan, the day of the festival of First Fruits. In fact, *Yeshua* is called the first fruits of those who rise from the dead.

1 Corinthians 15:20-23
But now Christ is risen from the dead, and has become the firstfruits of those who have fallen asleep. 21 For since by man came death, by Man also came the resurrection of the dead. 22 For as in Adam all die, even so in Christ all shall be made alive. 23 But each one in his own order: Christ the firstfruits, afterward those who are Christ's at His coming.

The Spiritual Understanding of First Fruits

Spiritual Application (Halacha). A sheaf in the Bible is used to typify a person or persons (Genesis 37:5-11). *Yeshua* will return to earth (*Zechariah 14:4*) during His second coming as King over all the earth. He also will bring the sheaves (the believers in *Yeshua* as the Messiah) with Him (Psalm 126; Jeremiah 31:9-14; Joel 3:11-13; Zechariah 14:3-5; Matthew 13:37-39; Mark 4:26-29; Hebrews 12:1; Jude 14; Revelation 1:7).

The 144,000 Jewish witnesses who witness of *Yeshua* during the *Chevlai shel Mashiach*, the birthpangs of the Messiah (also known as the tribulation) are first fruits to God during the tribulation (Revelation 14:1-4).

Let's look at some Scriptures in the Bible concerning first fruits.

1. The natural is before the spiritual (1 Corinthians 15:46).
2. Israel was God's firstborn (Exodus 4:22).
3. The gospel was preached to the Jew first and then to the non-Jews (Romans 1:16; 2:9-10; Matthew 10:5-6; 15:21-28; Acts 1:8).
4. We are called to seek first the Kingdom of God (Matthew 6:33).
5. *Yeshua* was the first to rise from the dead (Acts 26:23).
6. The early believers were a kind of first fruits (James 1:17-18).
7. Those who arose from the dead with *Yeshua* during His resurrection became the first fruits of all those who would rise from the dead (Matthew 27:52-53; Ephesians 4:8; 1 Thessalonians 4:13-18).

8. *Yeshua* first loved us, and He is to be our first love (1 John 4:9; Revelation 2:4).
9. *Yeshua* is the first (*Aleph*) and the last (*Tav*) (Revelation 1:8,11,17; 22:13; Isaiah 41:4; 44:6; 48:12).

Chapter 4
Pentecost

Shavuot

The Bible Names for the Feast of Pentecost are –Feast of Harvest-Feast of Weeks (Shavuot) – The Day of the First Fruits. The word Pentecost means 50 days- Shavuot is the celebration of the giving of the Law-The institution of the Nation of Israel and the pattern given for the Tabernacle— Celebrated 50 days after the Passover lamb was slain for their redemption from Egypt and the offering of the first fruits and the counting of the Omer for 49 Days.

Leviticus 23:9-18
*And the LORD spoke to Moses, saying,10 "Speak to the children of Israel, and say to them:'When you come into the land which I give to you, and reap its harvest, then you shall bring **a sheaf** (omer)of the firstfruits of your harvest to the priest.11 He shall wave the sheaf before the LORD, to be accepted on your behalf; on the day after the Sabbath the priest shall wave it.12 And you shall offer on that day, when you wave the sheaf, a male lamb of the first year, without blemish, as a burnt offering to the LORD.13 Its grain*

offering shall be two-tenths of an ephah of fine flour mixed with oil, an offering made by fire to the LORD, for a sweet aroma; and its drink offering shall be of wine, one-fourth of a hin.14 You shall eat neither bread nor parched grain nor fresh grain until the same day that you have brought an offering to your God; it shall be a statute forever throughout your generations in all your dwellings. 15 And you shall count for yourselves from the day after the Sabbath, from the day that you brought the sheaf of the wave offering: seven Sabbaths shall be completed.16 Count fifty days to the day after the seventh Sabbath; then you shall offer a new grain offering to the LORD.17 You shall bring from your dwellings two wave loaves of two-tenths of an ephah. They shall be of fine flour; they shall be baked with leaven. They are the firstfruits to the LORD.

How can we count the Omer now? And what can we offer to the Lord now?

Romans 12:1-2
I beseech you therefore, brethren, by the mercies of God, that you present your bodies a living sacrifice, holy, acceptable to God, which is your reasonable service.2 And do not be conformed to this world, but be transformed by the renewing of your mind, that you may prove what is that good and acceptable and perfect will of God.

Exodus 32:15-17
15 And Moses turned and went down from the mountain, and the two tablets of the Testimony were in his hand. The tablets were written on both sides; on the one side and on the other they were written.16 Now the tablets were the work of God,

and the writing was the writing of God engraved on the tablets. 17 And when Joshua heard the noise of the people as they shouted, he said to Moses, "There is a noise of war in the camp."

Exodus 32:25-28

Verse 25- Now when Moses saw that the people were unrestrained (for Aaron had not restrained them, to their shame among their enemies),26 then Moses stood in the entrance of the camp, and said, "Whoever is on the LORD's side -- come to me!" And all the sons of Levi gathered themselves together to him.27 And he said to them, "Thus says the LORD God of Israel: 'Let every man put his sword on his side, and go in and out from entrance to entrance throughout the camp, and let every man kill his brother, every man his companion, and every man his neighbor.'"28 So the sons of Levi did according to the word of Moses. And ***about three thousand men of the people fell that day.***

Solomon's Temple showed a pattern for the Day of Pentecost

2 Chronicles 5:12-14

12 and the Levites who were the singers, all those of Asaph and Heman and Jeduthun, with their sons and their brethren, stood at the east end of the altar, clothed in white linen, having cymbals, stringed instruments and harps, and with them ***one hundred and twenty priests*** *sounding with trumpets --13 indeed it came to pass, when the trumpeters and singers* ***were as one****, to make one sound to be heard in praising and thanking the LORD, and when they lifted up their voice with the trumpets and cymbals and instruments of music, and praised the LORD, saying: "For He is good, For*

His mercy endures forever," that the house, **the house of the LORD, was filled with a cloud,14 so that the priests could not continue ministering because of the cloud; for the glory of the LORD filled the house of God.**

Acts 2:41
"41 Then those who gladly received his word were baptized; **and that day about three thousand souls were added to them.**

If you look at Exodus 32:38 you will discover that when the law was given three thousand people died because of their sin. On the day of Pentecost when God sent His Holy Spirit, three thousand people lived instead of died. They were forgiven of their sins. Acts 2:41 records that three thousand people were added to the church on that day.

John1:17
"For the law was given through Moses, but grace and truth came through Jesus Christ."

When the Law was given on Shavuot – Pentecost – 3,000 people died because they broke the laws of God When the Holy Spirit was given at Shavuot – Pentecost – 3,000 people lived

Ephesians 2:14-18
For He Himself is our peace, who has made both one, and has broken down the middle wall of separation,15 having abolished in His flesh the enmity, that is, the law of commandments contained in ordinances, **so as to create in Himself one new man from the two**, *thus making peace,16 and that He might reconcile them both to God in one body*

through the cross, thereby putting to death the enmity. 17 And He came and preached peace to you who were afar off and to those who were near. 18 For through Him we both have access by one Spirit to the Father.

Ruach Ha Kodesh (the Holy Spirit)

Ezekiel prophesied of the Day when God would put His law in the hearts of His people by His Spirit

Ezekiel 36:26-31
26 I will give you a new heart and put a new spirit within you; I will take the heart of stone out of your flesh and give you a heart of flesh. 27 I will put My Spirit within you and cause you to walk in My statutes, and you will keep My judgments and do them. 28 Then you shall dwell in the land that I gave to your fathers; you shall be My people, and I will be your God. 29 I will deliver you from all your uncleanness. I will call for the grain and multiply it, and bring no famine upon you. 30 And I will multiply the fruit of your trees and the increase of your fields, so that you need never again bear the reproach of famine among the nations.

Acts 1:8
8 But you shall receive power when the Holy Spirit has come upon you; and you shall be witnesses to Me in Jerusalem, and in all Judea and Samaria, and to the end of the earth."

Acts 1:15
*And in those days Peter stood up in the midst of the disciples (altogether the number of names was about **a hundred and twenty**),*

Acts 2:1-4

*When the Day of Pentecost had fully come, they **were all with one accord in one place. 2 And suddenly there came a sound from heaven, as of a rushing mighty wind, and it filled the whole house where they were sitting.** 3 Then there appeared to them divided tongues, as of fire, and one sat upon each of them. 4 And they were all filled with the Holy Spirit and began to speak with other tongues, as the Spirit gave them utterance.*

John 15:26

"But when the Helper comes, whom I shall send to you from the Father, the Spirit of truth who proceeds from the Father, He will testify of Me." John 15:26

John 14:15-17

"If you love Me, keep My commandments. 16 And I will pray the Father, and He will give you another Helper, that He may abide with you forever -- 17 the Spirit of truth, whom the world cannot receive, because it neither sees Him nor knows Him; but you know Him, for He dwells with you and will be in you."

Not only did He send the Holy Spirit, but He sent Him to dwell in us. The world cannot have the Holy Spirit dwelling in them unless they receive Yeshua Ha Mashiach (Jesus The Messiah) into their lives and become born again. How do you think Jesus comes into a person's life and dwells in them? By the Holy Spirit. He doesn't unzip your body somewhere and try to fit His physical body in you somehow. Instead The Holy Spirit comes and joins with your spirit when you repent of your sins and accept what Jesus did for you on the cross. He took the punishment of our sins on

Himself. We should have died for our own sins. We are the guilty ones. But He chose to take our place and our punishment. His shed blood paid the price so you could come back into relationship with God.

Once Yeshua is living in your life you will have a relationship with God and not just religion. Having said all that. When Yeshua walked on the earth He healed the sick, He raised the dead, He worked signs, wonders and miracles. Every location He went miracles took place. He breathed on His disciples and they received the Holy Spirit and God began to work miracles through them. But they were only a few people.

By sending the Holy Spirit into the lives of every believer, Jesus life and ministry is duplicated. Everywhere people who are filled with the Holy Spirit go - miracles, signs and wonders should take place. **The very things Yeshua did is multiplied over and over again and in multiple lives and locations.**

I am so thankful that Yeshua sent Ruach Ha Kodesh on Pentecost (Shavuot) because now His laws are written in my heart. Now I have the power to live for God and to walk with Him. Now I don't have to fear that somehow I won't be good enough to spend eternity with Him. I don't have to die because of my sins. Instead I have life and that more abundantly.

John 10:10
"The thief does not come except to steal, and to kill, and to destroy. I have come that they may have life, and that they may have it more abundantly." - Yeshua

Chapter 5

The Feast of Trumpets

Rosh Hashanah

The name "Rosh Hashanah" is not used in the Bible. The Bible refers to the holiday as Yom Ha-Zikkaron (the day of remembrance) or Yom Teruah (the day of the sounding of the shofar). The origin of this holiday is found in Leviticus.

24 "Speak to the children of Israel, saying: 'In the seventh month, on the first day of the month, you shall have a sabbath-rest, a memorial of blowing of trumpets, a holy convocation. 25 You shall do no customary work on it; and you shall offer an offering made by fire to the LORD.'" Leviticus 23:24,25

The common greeting at this time is L'shanah tovah ("for a good year"). This is a shortening of "L'shanah tovah tikatev v'taihatem" (or to women, "L'shanah tovah tikatevi v'taihatemi"), which means "May you be inscribed and sealed for a good year."

The term "May you be inscribed" has to do with your name being written in the Book of Life. This holiday begins "The Ten Days of Awe." The ten days between Rosh Hashanah and Yom Kippur (Day of Atonement) is very important to the Jewish people. It is during these ten days that many Jewish people will seek to make things right with other people and give charitably to others to prepare themselves for Yom Kippur where they must make things right with God. All of this so they can be assured that their name is inscribed in the Book of life for the coming year.

The book of Revelation in the New Testament speaks of The Book of Life. It refers to it as "The Lamb's Book of Life."

Revelation 21:10
"And he carried me away in the Spirit to a great and high mountain, and showed me the great city, the holy Jerusalem, descending out of heaven from God."

Revelation 21:22-27
But I saw no temple in it, for the Lord God Almighty and the Lamb are its temple.23 The city had no need of the sun or of the moon to shine in it, for the glory of God illuminated it. The Lamb is its light.24 And the nations of those who are saved shall walk in its light, and the kings of the earth bring their glory and honor into it. 25 Its gates shall not be shut at all by day(there shall be no night there).26 And they shall bring the glory and the honor of the nations into it. 27 But there shall by no means enter it anything that defiles, or causes an abomination or a lie, **but only those who are written in the Lamb's Book of Life.**

Who are those who are written in The Lamb's Book of Life? Verse 24 refers to *"The nations of those who are saved"* If you are saved your name is written in The Lamb's Book of Life. Yeshua (Jesus) assures us that our names are written.

Luke 10:18-20
18 And He said to them, "I saw Satan fall like lightning from heaven. 19 Behold, I give you the authority to trample on serpents and scorpions, and over all the power of the enemy, and nothing shall by any means hurt you. 20 Nevertheless do not rejoice in this, that the spirits are subject to you, but rather **rejoice because your names are written in heaven.***"*

Why don't you rejoice right now? You do not have to worry about your name being written. If Yeshua is your Messiah and you have been Born Again, Your name is written.

Revelation 3:5
"He who overcomes shall be clothed in white garments, and I will not blot out his name from **the Book of Life***; but I will confess his name before My Father and before His angels."*

The Jewish New Year

Judaism has several different "new years," a concept which may seem strange at first, but think of it this way: the Gregorian calendar "new year" starts in January, In some places the "school year" starts in September, and many businesses have "fiscal years" that start at various times of the year. In Judaism, Nissan 1 is the new year for the purpose of counting the reign of kings and months on the calendar, Elul 1 (in August) is the new year for the tithing of animals, Shevat 15 (in February) is the new year for trees (determining when first fruits can be eaten, etc.), and Tishri 1 (Rosh Hashanah) is the new year for years (when we increase the year number. Sabbatical and Jubilee years begin at this time).

Some of the practices on Rosh Hashanah:

1. The Blowing of the Shofar
2. Tashlikh ("casting off").
3. Eating Apples & Honey, sweet cakes
4. Round Shaped Loaf, Ladder Shaped Loaf, Bird Shape Loaf (Isaiah 31:5)
5. Repentance, forgiveness, reconciliation
6. Giving to the poor

Jewish Tradition teaches that the following happened on Tishri 1:

1. Adam & Eve were created
2. The flood waters dried up
3. Enoch was taken by God
4. Sarah and Rachel conceived
5. Samuel was conceived
6. Joseph Freed from prison by Pharoah
7. The forced labor of Hebrews in Egypt ended
8. Job contracted leprosy
9. Start of sacrifices on the altar Ezra built

The Shofar – The Feast of Trumpets

On Rosh HaShanah, The shofar is the primary trumpet. According to Leviticus 23:24 and Numbers 29, Rosh HaShanah is the day of the blowing of the trumpets. The original name is Yom (Day) Teruah (The staccato sound of the horn, which also means Shout). According to the Mishnah (Rosh HaShanah 16a, 3:3), the trumpet used for this purpose is the ram's horn, not trumpets made of metal as in

Numbers 10. On Rosh HaShanah, a shofar delivers the first blast, a silver trumpet the second, and then the shofar the third. On Rosh Hashanah the shofar is sounded one hundred times. The shofar represents our cry to God.

The Sounds of The Shofar

There are different types of sounds made by the Shofar which carry different meanings. These are some of the sounds used today in worship.

Tekiah: A low to high pitch transition starting with a hard short push on the low pitch and then a slight sustain on the high pitch ending with a burst. Signifying God as king

Shevarim: Three short low to high pitch notes in a row. It is like three short tekiahs without the burst at the end. Signifying being broken before God

Teru'ah: Nine staccato notes or more blown in rapid succession at a medium pitch. Signifying a cry for mercy also used to shout with victory and jubilee when that mercy is received. Also used as a call to arms a warning of impending danger

Shevarim-Teru'ah: The combination of the last two sounds. Signifying Repentance and a turning away from your sin

Tekiah Gedolah: (The Great Blast) A long drawn out note held as long as possible. Starting out with the low to high pitch and ending with a burst. Signifying the drawing of God's people to himself. Based on Exodus 19:13 "When the shofar sounds long, They [the People] shall come up the mountain."

Yom Kippur (The Day of Atonement) which takes place 10 days later is ended at sundown with the Tekiah Gedolah shofar call.

The Shofar is blown once before the Rosh Hashanah service, six times during, and once after, the shofar is blown in the following order (a tekiah gedolah replaces the final tekiah in the set blown before musaf):

Tekiah, shevarim, teruah, tekiah
Tekiah, shevarim, teruah, tekiah
Tekiah, shevarim, teruah, tekiah

Tekiah, shevarim, tekiah
Tekiah, shevarim, tekiah
Tekiah, shevarim, tekiah

Tekiah, teruah, tekiah
Tekiah, teruah, tekiah
Tekiah, teruah, tekiah

This formula is repeated twice, making thirty sounds for the series. The last tekiah is prolonged and is called tekiah gedolah. This series of thirty sounds is repeated twice, making ninety sounds in all. The series is based on the mention of teruah three times in connection with the seventh month (Leviticus 23,24, and Numbers 29), In addition a single formula of ten sounds is rendered at the close of the service, making a total of 100 sounds.

Conclusion

The Jewish people do all these things for Ten days from Rosh Hashanah to Yom Kippur to make things right with others and with God so they can assure that their name will be written in the book of life. But Yeshua took our punishment for our sins and paid the price. It is because of His atonement for sin that our names are written in the Lamb's book of life.

2 Corinthians 5:21

For He made Him who knew no sin to be sin for us, that we might become the righteousness of God in Him.

I believe that we should seek to make things right with people and with God every day of our lives. Not just for ten days. Not so we can get our name written in the book of life. But instead so we can always be in right standing with others and with God.

Chapter 6
The Day of Atonement

Yom Kippur

Yom Kippur (Jewish Perspective)

Yom Kippur is probably the most important holiday of the Jewish year. Many Jews who do not observe any other Jewish custom will refrain from work, fast and/or attend synagogue services on this day. Yom Kippur occurs on the 10th day of Tishri The holiday is instituted at Leviticus 23:26

The name "Yom Kippur" means "Day of Atonement," and that pretty much explains what the holiday is. It is a day set aside to "afflict the soul," to atone for the sins of the past year.

During "the Days of Awe" according to Jewish tradition God inscribes all of our names in the Book of Life. On Yom Kippur, the judgment entered in these books is sealed. This day is, essentially, your last appeal, your last chance to change the judgment, to demonstrate your repentance and make amends.

Yom Kippur atones only for sins between man and God, not for sins against another person. To atone for sins against another person, you must first seek reconciliation with that person, righting the wrongs you committed against them if possible. That must all be done before Yom Kippur.

Yom Kippur is a complete Sabbath; no work can be performed on that day. It is well-known that you are supposed to refrain from eating and drinking (even water) on Yom Kippur. It is a complete, 25-hour fast beginning before sunset on the evening before Yom Kippur and ending after nightfall on the day of Yom Kippur. The Five Prohibitions of Yom Kippur are: Eating and drinking, anointing with perfumes or lotions, marital relations ,washing,wearing leather shoes.As always, any of these restrictions can be lifted where a threat to life or health is involved. In fact, children under the age of nine and women in childbirth (from the time labor begins until three days after birth) are not permitted to fast, even if they want to. Older children and women from the third to the seventh day after childbirth are permitted to fast, but are permitted to break the fast if they feel the need to do so.

Most of the holiday is spent in the synagogue in prayer. In Orthodox synagogues, services begin early in the morning (8 or 9 AM) and continue until about 3 PM. People then usually go home for an afternoon nap and return around 5 or 6 PM for the afternoon and evening services, which continue until nightfall. The services end at nightfall, with the blowing of the tekiah gedolah, a long blast on the shofar.

.

It is customary to wear white on the holiday, which symbolizes purity and calls to mind the promise that our sins shall be made as white as snow (Is. 1:18). Some people wear a kittel, the white robe in which the dead are buried

Yom Kippur (Christian Perspective)

Hebrews 9:6-8

"Now when these things had been thus prepared, the priests always went into the first part of the tabernacle, performing the services. 7 But into the second part the high priest went alone once a year, not without blood, which he offered for himself and for the people's sins committed in ignorance;"

Hebrews 9:11-14

*"But Christ came as High Priest of the good things to come, with the greater and more perfect tabernacle not made with hands, that is, not of this creation. 12 Not with the blood of goats and calves, but with His own blood He entered the Most Holy Place **once for all**, having obtained eternal redemption. 13 For if the blood of bulls and goats and the ashes of a heifer, sprinkling the unclean, sanctifies for the purifying of the flesh, 14 how much more shall the blood of Christ, who through the eternal Spirit offered Himself without spot to God, cleanse your conscience from dead works to serve the living God?"*

Hebrews 10:19-20

*"19Therefore, brethren, having boldness to enter the Holiest by the blood of Jesus, 20 by a new and living way which He consecrated for us, **through the veil, that is, His flesh,"***

Think about the fact that the High Priest could only enter the Holy of Holies once a year. It was on the Day of Atonement. And the application of the blood of animals only covered the sins of the people but did not permanently remove their sins.

Now think about the fact that Yeshua entered the Holy of Holies with His own blood and removed our sins forever. He does not have to do this anymore. It is done. It is finished. Also think about the fact that now you and I have access to the Holy of Holies to be able to experience the manifest presence of God every day of our lives because of the blood of Yeshua. What a joy and a privilege we have. A privilege that many take for granted. Our Day of Atonement took place on the cross of Calvary. Yeshua's last words were "It is finished".

I want to ask you right now. Have you received the benefits of this finished work into your life? Have you accepted what Yeshua (Jesus) did for you? If you know you are not right with God and you want to be, then now is the time to stop and ask Him to cleanse you from all your sins and put you in right standing with Him. This cannot be done by your good works. It can only be done by accepting the finished work He accomplished for you through His death and resurrection.

Why don't you pray this prayer out loud right now and make these confessions

God let my prayer come before You, and do not hide Yourself from me. What can I say to You The Almighty God? You know all things, both hidden and revealed. You search my heart and thoughts. Nothing is hidden from Your sight. I am not so arrogant nor hardened to say, "I am righteous and have not sinned." For I have sinned. I have not kept all Your commandments. You are righteous and true in all Your ways, but I have done evil in Your sight. Thank You God that You forgive all my sins, pardon all my iniquities, and grant atonement for all my transgressions through Yeshua the Messiah. For it is written: If we confess our sins, He is faithful and just to forgive us our sins and to cleanse us from all unrighteousness.

Lord please forgive me and cleanse me with your blood. I repent:

For the sins I've committed in Your sight by sinning willfully, and for the sins I committed in ignorance.

For the sin I've committed in Your sight by slander, and for the sin of gossip.

For the sin I've committed in Your sight by neglecting my responsibilities, and for the sin of selfishness.

For the sin I've committed in Your sight by indulging evil thoughts, and for the sin of lust.

For the sin I've committed in Your sight by being lukewarm, and for the sin of not loving You with all my heart and soul.

For the sin I've committed in Your sight by not hungering and thirsting for righteousness, and for the sin of not putting You first in my life.

For the sin I've committed in Your sight by not being merciful, and for the sin of withholding when I could have given.

For the sin I've committed in Your sight by speaking foolish words, and for the sin of not controlling my tongue.

For the sin I've committed in Your sight by not loving my neighbors, and for the sin of not blessing my enemies.

For the sin I've committed in Your sight by not turning the other cheek, and for the sin of practicing my own righteousness before others.

For the sin I've committed in Your sight by being proud, and for the sin of lack of zeal.

For the sin I've committed in Your sight knowingly, and for the sin I've committed unknowingly. For all these, O God of forgiveness, forgive me, pardon me, and grant me atonement in Yeshua the Messiah.

For the sin I've committed in Your sight by not walking as Yeshua walked, and for the sin of not being filled with Your Spirit.

For the sin I've committed in Your sight by loving the world, and for the sin of loving the things in the world.

For the sin I've committed in Your sight by putting other things before You, and for the sin of idolatry.

For the sin I've committed in Your sight by not praying at all times, and for the sin of not being thankful.

For the sin I've committed in Your sight by not being quick to forgive, and for the sin of holding resentments.

For the sin I've committed in Your sight by not going the second mile, and for the sin of impatience.

For the sin I've committed in Your sight by not doing unto others as we would have them do unto us, and for the sin of greed.

For the sin I've committed in Your sight by being anxious about the things of this life, and for the sin of not trusting You to provide for all of my needs.

For the sin I've committed in Your sight by setting my mind on the things below, and for the sin of not setting my mind on things above.

For all these, O God of forgiveness, forgive me, pardon me, and grant me atonement in Yeshua the Messiah. I truly repent from My heart and I turn away from all these things – In Yeshua's Name I pray.

Chapter 7
The Feast of Tabernacles

Sukkot

Leviticus 23:33-36,39-43

The Feast of Tabernacles is a week-long autumn harvest festival. Tabernacles is also known as the Feast of the Ingathering, Feast of the Booths, Sukkoth, Succoth, or Sukkot (variations in spellings occur because these words are transliterations of the Hebrew word pronounced "Sue-coat"). The two days following the festival are separate holidays, Shemini Atzeret and Simkhat Torah, but are commonly thought of as part of the Feast of Tabernacles.

The Feast of Tabernacles was the final and most important holiday of the year. The importance of this festival is indicated by the statement, "This is to be a lasting ordinance." The divine pronouncement, "I am the Lord your God," concludes this section on the holidays of the seventh month. The Feast of Tabernacles begins five days after Yom Kippur on the fifteenth of Tishri (September or October). It is a drastic change from one of the most solemn holidays in our year to one of the most joyous. The word Sukkoth means "booths," and refers to the temporary dwellings that Jews are commanded to live in during this holiday, just as the Jews did in the wilderness. The Feast of Tabernacles lasts for seven days and ends on the twenty-first day of the Hebrew month of Tishri, which is Israel's seventh month.

This holiday has a dual significance: historical and agricultural (just as Passover and Pentecost). Historically, it was to be kept in remembrance of the dwelling in tents in the wilderness for the forty-year period during which the children of Israel were wandering in the desert.

It is expounded in Leviticus 23:43 That your generations may know that I made the children of Israel to dwell in booths, when I brought them out of the land of Egypt: I am the LORD your God.

What were they to remember?

Many of the feasts were set in place to bring to remembrance the things that God has done for His people. When Sukkot is celebrated certain things were to be remembered:

1.) The humbleness of their beginning, and the low and desolate state out of which God advanced that people.

2.) The mercy of God to them, that, when they dwelt in tabernacles, God not only set up a tabernacle for Himself among them, but, with the utmost care and tenderness imaginable, hung a canopy over them, even the cloud that sheltered them from the heat of the sun. God's former mercies to us and our fathers ought to be kept in everlasting remembrance.

3.) The eighth day was the great day of this holiday, because then they returned to their own houses again, and remembered how, after they had long dwelt in tents in the wilderness, at length they came to a happy settlement in the land of promise, where they dwelt in goodly houses. And they would the more sensibly value and be thankful for the comforts and conveniences of their houses when they had been seven days dwelling in booths. It is good for those that have ease and plenty sometimes to learn what it is to endure hardness.

4.)They were to keep this holiday in thankfulness to God for all the increase of the year; however, the emphasis is that Israel's life rested upon redemption which in its ultimate meaning is the forgiveness of sin.

The word "**Sukkah**" means "**Tabernacle or Booth**"

The term "**Arba Minim**" refers to **The Four Species**

"**Lulav**"= Palm Fronds

"**Etrog**"= Fruit of Citrus Trees

"**Hadassim**" = Leafy branches

"**Aravot**" = Willows from the riverside

The Four Species were to remind Israel of the four stages of the wilderness journey:

1. The palm branches represented the valleys and the plains.
2. The citrus, reminded them of the good land the Lord had given.
3. The leafy branches represented the bushes on the mountains
4. The willows reminded them of the brooks where they drank

When Jesus walked on earth it is recorded many times His participation in the feasts. He gave new significance to the different aspects of the each feast. Each truth revealed, always pointed to Him and gave new revelation and insight into the different feasts.

Jesus Celebrated the Feast of Tabernacles

Jesus celebrated the Feast of Tabernacles. He taught in the Temple on the Feast of Tabernacles. Although His disciples had not expected Jesus to attend the feast, the vast majority of the pilgrims from afar who had heard of Him entertained the hope that they might see Him at Jerusalem. They were not disappointed, for on several occasions He taught in Solomon's Porch and elsewhere in the temple courts. These teachings were really the official or formal announcement of the divinity of Jesus to the Jewish people and to the whole world. Jesus risked His life to go to the Feast of Tabernacles, but the boldness of Jesus in publicly appearing in Jerusalem overawed his enemies; they were not prepared for such a daring challenge.

John 7:2-11

*2 Now the Jews' **Feast of Tabernacles** was at hand. 3 His brothers therefore said to Him, "Depart from here and go into Judea, that Your disciples also may see the works that You are doing. 4 For no one does anything in secret while he himself seeks to be known openly. If You do these things, show Yourself to the world." 5 For even His brothers did not believe in Him. 6 Then Jesus said to them, "My time has not yet come, but your time is always ready. 7 The world cannot hate you, but it hates Me because I testify of it that its works are evil. 8 You go up to this feast. I am not yet going up to this feast, for My time has not yet fully come." 9 When He had* *said these things to them, He remained in Galilee. 10 But when His brothers had gone up, then **He also went up to the feast**, not openly, but as it were in secret. 11 Then the Jews sought Him at the feast, and said, "Where is He?*

John 7:14-15
*14 Now about **the middle of the feast** Jesus went up into the temple and taught. 15 And the Jews marveled, saying, "How does this Man know letters, having never studied?"*

John 7:37-39
***On the last day, that great day of the feast**, Jesus stood and cried out, saying, "If anyone thirsts, let him come to Me and drink. 38 He who believes in Me, as the Scripture has said, out of his heart will flow rivers of living water." 39 But this He spoke concerning the Spirit, whom those believing in Him would receive; for the Holy Spirit was not yet given, because Jesus was not yet glorified.*

When Jesus stood up on the last day of the feast and began to proclaim *"If anyone thirsts, let him come to Me and drink."* He knew and everyone else knew that this was the time when the priest would pour water and quote Isaiah 12:2-6.

Jesus The Living Water

On the last day and greatest day of the Feast of Tabernacles (the day the Rabbis poured the water) Jesus stood (calling special attention to His message) and proclaimed Himself the very fountain of living water.

Our spiritual thirst can only be quenched by Yeshua.

John 4:13-14
"Whoever drinks of this water will thirst again, 14 but whoever drinks of the water that I shall give him will never thirst. But the water that I shall give him will become in him a fountain of water springing up into everlasting life."

"Simhat Bet Hasho'eva"

"Rejoicing of the Place of Water-Drawing"

On the last day of the feast a priest was sent to the Pool of Siloam with a golden pitcher to bring water to the foot of the altar where was a basin into which the water was poured. The pouring of water signified the prayer for abundant rain which was necessary for the growth of their crops.

When the priest would pour out the water he would quote:

Isaiah 12:2-6
2 Behold, God is my salvation, I will trust and not be afraid; 'For YAH, the LORD, is my strength and song; He also has become my salvation.'" 3 Therefore with joy you will draw water From the wells of salvation. 4 And in that day you will say: "Praise the LORD, call upon His name; Declare His deeds among the peoples, Make mention that His name is exalted. 5 Sing to the LORD, For He has done excellent things; This is known in all the earth. 6 Cry out and shout, O inhabitant of Zion, For great is the Holy one of Israel in your midst!"

Now re-read Isaiah 12:2-6 and every time you see the word "salvation" insert "Yeshua" Jesus name in Hebrew is – Yeshua , which translated means "salvation"

Save us now

Also on the last day of the feast the people would take the "Lulav" in their right hand and the "Etrog" in the left hand and shake them vigorously they would face the east, south, west and north and do this. They called this:

"**Hoshana Raba**" meaning "The Great Hosanna". Hosanna translated means: "Save us now"

This scripture was quoted during this prophetic act.

Psalm 118:25-29
25 Save now, I pray, O LORD; O LORD, I pray, send now prosperity.26 Blessed is he who comes in the name of the LORD! We have blessed you from the house of the LORD. 27 God is the LORD, And He has given us light; Bind the sacrifice with cords to the horns of the altar. 28 You are my God, and I will praise You; You are my God, I will exalt You. 29 Oh, give thanks to the LORD, for He is good! For His mercy endures forever.

This reminds us of when Jesus entered Jerusalem on a donkey and the people cried: "Hosanna" (save us now)

Matthew 21:6-9
6 So the disciples went and did as Jesus commanded them.7 They brought the donkey and the colt, laid their clothes on them, and set Him on them.8 And a very great multitude spread their clothes on the road; others cut down branches from the trees and spread them on the road.9 Then the

multitudes who went before and those who followed cried out, saying:"Hosanna to the Son of David!'Blessed is He who comes in the name of the LORD!'Hosanna in the highest!"

Messiah Ben Joseph, Messiah Ben David

Jewish scholars had concluded from the scriptures regarding the coming Messiah that there must be two messiahs. Messiah Ben Joseph and Messiah Ben David. Messiah Ben Joseph revealed in scripture was a suffering servant. Messiah Ben David the conquering king. It was hard to reconcile and understand that the two messiahs could actually be one person. We are reminded of the time Yeshua entered Jerusalem. The crowd cried out "Hosanna" (save us now). Why were they crying this? Because they were expecting Messiah Ben David. They were expecting that He was coming into Jerusalem to set up His kingdom. That is why they cried out "Hosanna"! When He didn't set up His kingdom, the same people not much later cried "Crucify Him". They didn't realize that Yeshua came first as Messiah Ben Joseph, the suffering Messiah. He declared:

John 18:36

"My kingdom is not of this world. If My kingdom were of this world, My servants would fight, so that I should not be delivered to the Jews; but now My kingdom is not from here."

He is coming again. He will set up His Kingdom. This time He will come as Messiah Ben David. The conquering messiah, The conquering king.

Yeshua is the Light of the World

There was something else very significant that happened during the Feast of Tabernacles that revealed Yeshua in this feast. At night time they would light four giant candelabras and bowls of oil that would illumine the temple and light the city – it was during this time that Jesus proclaimed:

John 8:12

*12 Then Jesus spoke to them again, saying, **"I am the light of the world**. He who follows Me shall not walk in darkness, but have the light of life."*

God is Our Shelter

This holiday reminds us not to hold too tightly to material things. We live in a very materialistic age. When the Israelites were wanderers in the desert, they all lived in tents– rich and poor alike. Material possessions can control and manipulate us; they become gods, or idols, over us. We must remember that this life is only temporary. We are also on a pilgrimage to a Promised Land in eternity. We need to seek God's kingdom, not earthly comfort. As we seek first the Kingdom of God (Luke 12:31), God is our shelter. For thou hast been a strength to the poor, a strength to the needy in his distress, a refuge from the storm, a shadow from the heat, when the blast of the terrible ones is as a storm against the wall (Isa. 25:4).

Jesus is Preparing Our Permanent Home

These physical bodies we now occupy are only temporary dwelling places. Our bodies are frail, and will eventually begin to deteriorate. Life is short. Our hope is not in what the world has to offer, but in what God has already provided for us for eternity. Our permanent home is being prepared for us in eternity. Jesus said in John 14:2-3, *In my Father's house are many mansions: if it were not so, I would have told you. I go to prepare a place for you. And if I go and prepare a place for you, I will come again, and receive you unto myself; that where I am, there ye may be also.*

As the Israelites left bondage, we leave the bondage of sin. God brought the Children of Israel out of the bondage of their Egyptian taskmasters into freedom. For Christians, we can celebrate that God redeemed us from a life of bondage to sin and brought us into His freedom in the Kingdom of God.

Was the first Thanksgiving a Feast of Tabernacles Celebration?

Many Americans, upon seeing a decorated sukkah for the first time, remark on how much the sukkah (and the holiday generally) reminds them of Thanksgiving. The American pilgrims, who originated the Thanksgiving holiday, were deeply religious people. As they were trying to find a way to express their thanks for their survival and for the harvest, it is quite possible that they looked to the Bible (Leviticus 23:39) for an appropriate way of celebrating and based their holiday in part on the Feast of Tabernacles. Note: celebrating Thanksgiving on the third Thursday of November was established by the American government and may not necessarily coincide with the pilgrim's first observance.

Was the Birth of Christ during the Feast of Tabernacles?

Many scholars believe Jesus was born during the Feast of Tabernacles. The Bible does not specifically say the date of Jesus' birth. We know it was not during the winter months because the sheep were in the pasture (Luke 2:8). A study of the time of the conception of John the Baptist reveals he was conceived about Sivan 30, the eleventh week. When Zechariah was ministering in the temple, he received an announcement from God of a coming son. The eighth course of Abia, when Zechariah was ministering, was the week of Sivan 12 to 18. Adding forty weeks for a normal pregnancy reveals that John the Baptist was born on or about Passover (Nisan 14). We know six months after John's conception, Mary conceived Jesus (Luke 1:26-33). Therefore, Jesus would have been conceived six months later in the month of Kislev. Kislev 25 is Hanukkah. Was the "light of the world" conceived on the festival of lights? Starting at Hanukkah, which begins on Kislev 25 and continues for eight days, and counting through the nine months of Mary's pregnancy, one arrives at the approximate time of the birth of Jesus at the Festival of Tabernacles (the early fall of the year).

During the Feast of Tabernacles, God required all male Jews to come to Jerusalem. The many people coming to Jerusalem for the festivals would spill over to the surrounding towns (Bethlehem is about five miles from Jerusalem). Joseph and Mary were unable to find a room at the inn because of the influx of so many people. They may have been given shelter in a sukkah, which is built during a seven-day period each year accompanying the celebration of the Feast of Tabernacles. Due to the difficulties during travel, it was common for the officials to declare tax time during a temple Feast (Luke 2:1). We know our Messiah was made manifest into a temporary body when He came to earth. Is it possible He also was put into a temporary dwelling? The fields would have been dotted with sukkahs during this harvest time to temporary shelter animals. The Hebrew word "stable" is called a sukkah (Gen. 33:17). And she brought forth her firstborn son, and wrapped him in swaddling clothes, and laid him in a manger; because there was no room for them in the inn (Luke 2:7). Joseph and Mary took the child and flew to Egypt and remained there until they were told by God that Herod was dead. Joseph and Mary brought the baby Jesus into Jerusalem forty days from His birth for Mary's purification and the child's dedication (according to Torah this had to be done within forty days of the birth of a male child–not doing so is considered a sin). This indicates that Herod died within the same forty days, because as long as Herod was alive, they could not appear at the Temple. (According to Josephus' calculations, Herod's death occurred during the Autumn in the fourth year before the Common Era 4 b.c.e.). Later in His life, Yeshua celebrated His birthday on a mountain with three of His disciples. In contrast to birthday parties, such as Herod's, where people were killed for entertainment, His was a celebration of life. On the Festival of Succoth, Moshe (Moses) and EliYahu (Elijah), from centuries past, representatives of the Torah and the Prophets, appeared and talked with Yeshua. One disciple, Kepha (Peter), suggested building three succoth for Yeshua, Moshe, and EliYahu, because it was required for the festival, but he did not understand that these three were fulfilling that which the festival symbolized: they were dwelling in their succoth (temporary tabernacles) of flesh, awaiting their eternal resurrection temples A number of Christians are celebrating Christ's birth during the Feast of Tabernacles, complete with decorations and lights on the sukkah, a birthday cake, and music celebrating Jesus' birth.

Is it wrong to celebrate Christmas on December 25th?

Celebrating the birth of the Messiah is not a bad thing. In fact celebrating and focusing on the life of Yeshua is a good thing. I enjoy celebrating Christmas with my family and others. It can be very meaningful to those who realize that Jesus is the reason for the season and that wise men still seek Him. The most important thing is that we should have an intimate relationship with Him every day. We should set our affections on things above and not on the things of this earth. We must fix our eyes on Jesus, the author and finisher of our faith. It is not the date that you celebrate His birth that is important. It is the fact that He came. We celebrate that God sent His only Son. Whoever believes in Him will not perish but have everlasting life.

For the people who get hung up on when we should be celebrating the birth of the Messiah, I say it is good to celebrate His birth during the Feast of Tabernacles and during Christmas. Why? Because Hanukkah the festival of lights usually falls close to December 25th and that is actually around the time Ruach Ha Kodesh (Holy Spirit) overshadowed Miriam (Mary) and Yeshua was conceived. The beginning a of a person's life is not when they finally come out of womb, but instead when they are conceived. Also because it is most likely that Yeshua came out of the womb during Sukkot we can celebrate His entrance into this world.

Thank you Yeshua for coming into this world for us.

Chapter 8
The Feast of Dedication

Hanukkah

The only reference to **Chanukah** , or **Hannukah,** in most bibles is where it is recorded that Jesus went to Jerusalem to celebrate it. (John 10: 22-23) The story of the events it celebrates is found in the book of 1 Macabees in the Apocrypha. The Apocrypha can be found in Roman Catholic Bibles and in one version of the New English Bible. Though the Apocrypha does not meet the criteria to be canonized and accepted as scripture the books contain historical records that record certain events in history.

Chanukah falls on 25th of Kislev on the Jewish calendar; in either November or December on the western calendar .

Chanukah is also known as the Feast of Lights or the Feast of Dedication.

Background

In 165 BCE the Greek empire, under Antiochus Epiphanes IV imposed Greek philosophy and religion on Israel and throughout the empire. They built an Image of their god Zeus on top of the Temple altar and desecrated the temple by sacrificing pigs. This fulfilled a prophesy in the book of Daniel. The abandonment of Jewish customs was enforced by terror.

A revolt led by Judah Macabee, in the manner of all God's miraculous deliverances, was successful in driving out the Greeks and the temple was cleansed and rededicated. However, it was found that there was only sufficient purified olive oil to light the *Menorah* (seven branch candelabra) in the Temple for one day and it would take eight days to purify further supplies. However, the *Menorah* (lampstand) burned miraculously until the fresh supplies were ready.

Celebration

Chanukah is celebrated for eight days, although normal work is permissible. Gifts are given each day of the celebration to the children, making it a very fun time. Games are played such as spinning the dreidel and chocolate coins with gold foil covering are given out to the children. Latkes (potato pancakes) are eaten. All these are traditions that have developed over the years.

The main celebration is the lighting of candles, or lamps in every home, That is why some call it the Festival of

Lights. A nine candle holder (The *Chanukiah*) is used, with an one extra candle being lit every day for eight days. The first night of Hanukkah begins with lighting the ninth candle which is called "the servant" (*ha shammash*) and is used to light one candle each night adding the amount of candles that coincide with how many nights the celebration has been celebrated totaling eight. The eight candles are set apart solely for the purpose of showing that you are commemorating the miracle of eight days of light provided by God to rededicate the sanctuary. That is why there are 44 candles in a box of Hanukkah candles because you must light each night the amount of candles including the ninth candle that parallels with the amount of days into the celebration. The "servant candle" is interesting to the Christian who remembers the suffering servant, messianic prophecies and the fact that Yeshua came to be the light of the World. See Isaiah 9:2, Isaiah 42:6, Isaiah 49:6, Isaiah 60 :1, Luke 2:32, John 1 :4,9 John 8:12.

Jesus Celebrated the Feast of Dedication

Not only did Jesus celebrate this feast, but He purposely did something during this feast that spoke of His deity and He being God.

John 10:22-33
Now it was the Feast of Dedication in Jerusalem, and it was winter. 23 And Jesus walked in the temple, in Solomon's porch. 24 Then the Jews surrounded Him and said to Him, "How long do You keep us in doubt? If You are the Christ, tell us plainly." 25 Jesus answered them, "I told you, and you

73

*do not believe. The works that I do in My Father's name, they bear witness of Me. 26 But you do not believe, because you are not of My sheep, as I said to you. 27 My sheep hear My voice, and I know them, and they follow Me. 28 And I give them eternal life, and they shall never perish; neither shall anyone snatch them out of My hand. 29 My Father, who has given them to Me, is greater than all; and no one is able to snatch them out of My Father's hand. 30 **I and My Father are one.** "Then the Jews took up stones again to stone Him. 32 Jesus answered them, "Many good works I have shown you from My Father. For which of those works do you stone Me?" 33 The Jews answered Him, saying, "For a good work we do not stone You, but for blasphemy, and because **You, being a Man, make Yourself God."***

Remember that Antiochus Epiphanes IV desecrated the altar and set Zeus up as God in the temple. This was the whole reason for the revolt and the need to retake the temple. The temple had to be retaken and consecrated and re-dedicated, making it holy once again. That is why Hanukkah is celebrated because of the dedication of the Temple and the miracle that God performed with the oil.

For Jesus to choose to go into the temple during this celebration and declare "I and My Father are one", hit a sore spot in the heart of every Jew present. To them Jesus was committing blasphemy just as Antiochus Epiphanes IV did. But the fact remains that Jesus was speaking the truth.

We are the Temples of the Holy Spirit

We can learn a lot from the celebration of Hanukkah – The Feast of Dedication.

I think of the analogy of re-dedicating the temple, consecrating and making it holy. Preparing holy oil to light the temple menorah. It makes me think about how we are the Temples of Ruach Ha Kodesh (The Holy Spirit). How we must consecrate and purify our lives to be holy so that God can fill our temples with His presence. Our desire should be that the light of our temples would shine forth Yeshua.

1 Corinthians 3:16-17
16 Do you not know that you are the temple of God and that the Spirit of God dwells in you? 17 If anyone defiles the temple of God, God will destroy him. For the temple of God is holy, which temple you are.

1 Corinthians 6:19-20
19 Or do you not know that your body is the temple of the Holy Spirit who is in you, whom you have from God, and you are not your own? 20 For you were bought at a price; therefore glorify God in your body and in your spirit, which are God's.

Chapter 9
The Feast of Esther

Purim

Purim is not a commanded feast like the feasts that were given to Moses recorded in the Torah. The Celebration of Purim is based on the events recorded in the Book of Esther. The word "Pur" means lot – it has to do with the casting of the lot which determined the day that the Jewish people were to be exterminated.

Esther 3:7
In the first month, which is the month of Nisan, in the twelfth year of King Ahasuerus, they cast Pur (that is, the lot), before Haman to determine the day and the month, until it fell on the twelfth month, which is the month of Adar.

The Book of Esther records the reason that Purim has been celebrated by the Jewish people throughout history.

Esther 9:26-28
26 So they called these days Purim, after the name Pur. Therefore, because of all the words of this letter, what they had seen concerning this matter, and what had happened to them, 27 the Jews established and imposed it upon themselves and their descendants and all who would join them, that

without fail they should celebrate these two days every year, according to the written instructions and according to the prescribed time, 28 that these days should be remembered and kept throughout every generation, every family, every province, and every city, that these days of Purim should not fail to be observed among the Jews, and that the memory of them should not perish among their descendants.

It is interesting that God is not mentioned once in the Book of Esther, but His involvement throughout the book is evident. It reminds us of the fact that even when we face and are going through difficult times and it seems like God is not there, that He is always with us working behind the scenes assuring and securing the victory for us. The Book of Esther is a story of great triumph for the Jewish people. The Jewish people were threatened with genocide but were miraculously delivered.

"Hag Purim, Hag Purim, Hag gadol shel yeladim." "The Feast of Purim, the Feast of Purim, a great holiday for the children," proclaims this little song. It resounds throughout the streets of Israel during the Purim celebration which is also called the Feast of Esther. At this holiday time, which falls in late February or early March (in the Hebrew month Adar), children run around costumed as beautiful Queen Esther, righteous Mordecai or regal King Ahasuerus. A festive mood prevails, creating infectious smiles on everyone's face.

Most other Jewish holidays carry a sense of solemnity and deep reverence, and any expressed joy is usually in the form of psalms and hymns. Purim, however, is different. In fact Purim is a time when the rabbis permit—even encourage—people to demonstrate their joy with such fervor that young and old alike may at times seem almost beside themselves with emotion.

Purim time is party time. Along with the costumes and gaiety, the more fortunate traditionally give charity and donations of food to the needy. As always at holiday times, special foods abound. Most popular are the little pastries called *ozneh Haman*, Haman's ears, or *Hamantaschen* which are supposed to represent Haman's three-cornered hat. The latter are triangular-shaped pastries that usually contain prune or poppy seed and honey fillings. These sweets are designed to remind us of the story of Purim as we recall how God turned the evil designs of wicked Haman into something good for the Jewish people.

The Hebrew word *Purim* means "lots," referring to Haman's casting of lots to determine the best time for murdering the Jews. During the Feast of Purim particular attention is paid to the events surrounding the holiday as recorded in the book of Esther. Traditionally the scroll must be read through at least once; but in many circles multiple readings are common. One Hasidic tradition teaches that the book of Esther should be read repeatedly throughout the entire night, or at least until the participants become so tired that they can no longer tell the difference between the name of Mordecai the hero and the name of Haman the villain.

The events that took place that are recorded in the Book of Esther were very important to the future establishment of the nation of Israel. Not only did God save His people from total destruction, but He forged relationships in the Persian Empire that would help in the restoration and rebuilding of Jerusalem.

King Ahasureus (Xerxes) began to rule Persia from 485 B.C. (this reign started in the fall of the year) In the 3rd year of his reign he threw a feast that lasted for 6 months (180 days) This is when Vashti was ousted as queen.

Esther 1:1-4

Now it came to pass in the days of Ahasuerus (this was the Ahasuerus who reigned over one hundred and twenty-seven provinces, from India to Ethiopia), 2 in those days when King Ahasuerus sat on the throne of his kingdom, which was in Shushan the citadel, 3 that in the third year of his reign he made a feast for all his officials and servants -- the powers of Persia and Media, the nobles, and the princes of the provinces being before him --4 when he showed the riches of his glorious kingdom and the splendor of his excellent majesty for many days, one hundred and eighty days in all.

This occured in the year 483-482 B.C. Hadassah (Hebrew name of Esther) was made queen in the 10th month in the seventh year of Xerxes reign.

Esther 2:16-18

So Esther was taken to King Ahasuerus, into his royal palace, in the tenth month, which is the month of Tebeth, in the seventh year of his reign. 17 The king loved Esther more than all the other women, and she obtained grace and favor in his sight more than all the virgins; so he set the royal crown upon her head and made her queen instead of Vashti. 18 Then the king made a great feast, the Feast of Esther, for all his officials and servants; and he proclaimed a holiday in the provinces and gave gifts according to the generosity of a king.

This means that it was in 478 B.C. God raised Esther up to save His people.

Esther 4:14

4 For if you remain completely silent at this time, relief and deliverance will arise for the Jews from another place, but you and your father's house will perish. Yet who knows whether you have come to the kingdom for such a time as this?"

Now let's jump to Nehemiah. Here we find that Nehemiah is the cup bearer to King Artaxerxes. Some questions that you should ask are:

1. Why would the king place a person from a conquered people as his cup bearer. The responsibility of a cup bearer was to protect the king from being poisoned. Not the position you want your enemy in?
2. Why was the king so interested in the feelings of a servant?

We have to start with King Xerxes to find the answer. Xerxes was killed in fall of 465 B.C. by Artabanus (his counseler) who also killed the oldest son (this was the son of Vashti). He then proclaimed himself king and was killed by Artaxerxes 1 several months later in hand to hand combat. Artaxerxes 1 was between 10 and 12 years old depending on the reference you check. This was quite a feat for a child that young but remember he was trained in combat since he was old enough to walk. Artaxerxes 1 then took the throne as the rightful king.

Esther the queen mother is still alive at this time. Now if Artaxerxes 1 is only 12 years old then he had to have been born in 477 B.C. This was the year following Esther becoming queen. So Esther was the mother of Artaxerxes 1 making him half Jewish. Now we see why he would have a Jew as a cup bearer. Not because it was a conquered people but because he was a Jew himself. In addition it was Artaxerxes 1 that in the 20th year of his reign (444 B.C.) issued the decree to rebuild Jerusalem

Jesus revealed in the Celebration of Purim

Mordecai and Esther both represent a type of Christ. Mordecai was falsely accused and destined to die. The very gallows that were intended to kill him were the very gallows that killed his enemy. Although Mordecai did not die on the gallows like Jesus died on the cross. The very cross that was intended to destroy Jesus ended up destroying His enemy.

1 Corinthians 2:8
"Which none of the rulers of this age knew; for had they known, they would not have crucified the Lord of glory."

1 John 3:8
For this purpose the Son of God was manifested, that He might destroy the works of the devil.

Also in the end Mordecai was placed in an exalted position.

Esther 10:2-3
2 Now all the acts of his power and his might, and the account of the greatness of Mordecai, to which the king advanced him, are they not written in the book of the chronicles of the kings of Media and Persia? 3 For Mordecai the Jew was second to King Ahasuerus, and was great among the Jews and well received by the multitude of his brethren, seeking the good of his people and speaking peace to all his countrymen.

Jesus is exalted to His rightful position:

Philippians 2:9-11
Therefore God also has highly exalted Him and given Him the name which is above every name, 10 that at the name of Jesus every knee should bow, of those in heaven, and of those on earth, and of those under the earth, 11 and that every tongue should confess that Jesus Christ is Lord, to the glory of God the Father.

Esther was also a type of Christ for she rose out of obscurity to intervene and save her people. Jesus was born in humble circumstances but rose to deliver all people from the wages of sin which is death. After 3 days of fasting Esther rose to intercede and bring deliverance to her people. After 3 days in the tomb, Jesus rose as the Savior of all mankind. Esther spoiled Haman's plot. Jesus spoiled the devils plot. The Book of Esther is a book of salvation. It tells the story of salvation. Yeshua is our Salvation!

Chapter 10

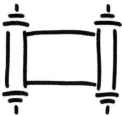

Other Feasts and Celebrations

There are other feasts and celebrations that are celebrated by the Jewish people that teach us biblical principles and point to Yeshua.

Tisha B'Av
(the 9th of Av)

Tisha B'av is not a celebration. Actually it is a day of mourning. Many bad things have happened to the Jewish people on this day. The fast commemorates the destruction of the First and Second Temples in Jerusalem, which occurred about 656 years apart, but on the same date. The day has been called the "saddest day in Jewish history". Tisha B'Av falls in July or August in the Gregorian calendar.

There are five events that took place on the 9th of Av that are the main focus, but there are also other events in history that happened on the 9th of Av that are remembered.

The Five Calamities

1. The 12 spies sent by Moses to observe the promised land returned from their mission. Two of the spies, Joshua and Caleb brought a positive report, but the others spoke evil about the land which caused the Children of Israel to cry, panic and despair of ever entering the "Promised Land". For this, they were punished by God that their generation would not enter the land. Because of the Israelites' lack of faith, God decreed that for all generations this date would become one of crying and misfortune for their descendants, the Jewish people. (See Numbers Chapters 13 & 14)

2. The First Temple built by Solomon was destroyed by the Babylonians led by Nebuchadnezzar in 586 BCE and the Jews were sent into the Babylonian exile.

3. The Second Temple was destroyed by the Romans in 70 AD, scattering the Jewish people which started the exile of the Jews from the Holy Land.

4. 135 AD - The Romans defeat Bar Kochba's last fortress, Betar, and destroy his army. Bar Kochba himself is killed along with more than 100,000 other Jews. The Roman Emperor Hadrian turns Jerusalem into a Roman city.

5. Following the Roman siege of Jerusalem, the destruction of Jerusalem occurred the next year. A temple was built in its stead to an idol.

Other calamities associated with Tisha B'Av:

- 1290 - The ninth of Av also happens to be the day that Jews were expelled from England

- 1492 - King Ferdinand and Queen Isabella expelled the Jews from Spain in

- 1914 - World War I begins when Germany declares war on Russia, setting the stage for World War II and the Holocaust.

- 1940 - Himmler presents his plan for the "Final Solution" to the Jewish problem to the Nazi Party.

- 1942 - Nazis begin deporting Jews from the Warsaw Ghetto.

.

When this day comes around every year I pray for my people that they will receive Yeshua as their Messiah. Yeshua can break every curse and break a pattern of bad and destructive experiences. No longer does the 9th of Av have to be a day when bad things happen.

Galatians 3:10-14

For as many as are of the works of the law are under the curse; for it is written, "Cursed is everyone who does not continue in all things which are written in the book of the law, to do them." 11 But that no one is justified by the law in the sight of God is evident, for "the just shall live by faith." 12 Yet the law is not of faith, but "the man who does them shall live by them." 13 Christ has redeemed us from the curse of the law, having become a curse for us (for it is written, "Cursed is everyone who hangs on a tree"),14 that the blessing of Abraham might come upon the Gentiles in Christ Jesus, that we might receive the promise of the Spirit through faith.

The Jews mourn the destruction of the Temple. The Temple was the center of the sacrificial system. This system was set up by God to atone for the sins of the people. The temple is no longer needed because Yeshua became the Lamb of God who takes away the sins of the world. If fact Yeshua referred to Himself as the Temple.

John 2:19-21

19 Jesus answered and said to them, "Destroy this temple, and in three days I will raise it up." 20 Then the Jews said, "It has taken forty-six years to build this temple, and will You raise it up in three days?"21 But He was speaking of the temple of His body.22 Therefore, when He had risen from the dead, His disciples remembered that He had said this to them; and they believed the Scripture and the word which Jesus had said.

Hebrews 9:11-15
But Christ came as High Priest of the good things to come,
with the greater and more perfect tabernacle not made with
hands, that is, not of this creation. 12 Not with the blood of
goats and calves, but with His own blood He entered the
Most Holy Place once for all, having obtained eternal
redemption. 13 For if the blood of bulls and goats and the
ashes of a heifer, sprinkling the unclean, sanctifies for the
purifying of the flesh, 14 how much more shall the blood of
Christ, who through the eternal Spirit offered Himself
without spot to God, cleanse your conscience from dead
works to serve the living God? 15 And for this reason He is
the Mediator of the new covenant, by means of death, for the
redemption of the transgressions under the first covenant,
that those who are called may receive the promise of the
eternal inheritance.

Yeshua has not just covered our sins, but He has
removed them. The sacrifice of His life and the shedding of
His blood was only necessary *"once for all"* That is why
God allowed the temple to be destroyed in AD 70. And that
is why it has never been built again and the sacrificial system
never re-established. Redemption is available for all people.

Simchat Torah
(Rejoicing in the Torah)

Leviticus 23:36
For seven days you shall offer an offering made by fire to the
LORD. On the Eighth day you shall have a holy convocation,
and you shall offer an offering made by fire to the LORD. It
is a sacred assembly, and you shall do no customary work on
it

Tishri 22, the day after the seventh day of Sukkot, is the holiday Shemini Atzeret. Which is also known as Simchat Torah. Shemini Atzeret literally means "the assembly of the eighth (day) Simchat Torah means "Rejoicing in the Torah." This holiday marks the completion of the annual cycle of weekly Torah readings. Each week in the synagogue a few chapters of the Torah are publicly read starting with Genesis Chapter 1 and ending on the last chapter of Deuteronomy . On Simchat Torah, the last portion of the Torah is read and then the first chapter of Genesis, as a reminder that the Torah is a circle, and never ends. This completion of the readings is a time of great celebration. There are processions around the synagogue carrying Torah scrolls and plenty of high-spirited singing and dancing in the synagogue with the Torahs. As many people as possible are given the honor of an aliya (reciting a blessing over the Torah reading); in fact, even children are called for an aliyah blessing on Simchat Torah. In addition, as many people as possible are given the honor of carrying a Torah scroll in these processions.

Yeshua is the living Word – We can rejoice and celebrate and thank God. We hide His word in our heart, but we don't keep it hidden. Instead we can bring it forth and let the world see and experience the living Word of God. We can give as many people as possible the honor of handling and carrying the Word of God.

John 1:1
In the beginning was the Word, and the Word was with God, and the Word was God.

John 1:14
And the Word became flesh and dwelt among us, and we beheld His glory, the glory as of the only begotten of the Father, full of grace and truth.

John 1:17
For the law was given through Moses, but grace and truth came through Jesus Christ.

Book Conclusion

I pray that this book has been a blessing to you. I pray that many nuggets of truth were imparted into your life. I have learned and gained much insight from the celebrations of the feasts of Israel. I have found that everything points to Yeshua (Jesus) the Messiah. My prayer is that this book has drawn you closer to Him and has given you a hunger to dig deeper. I know that there is many more insights and revelations that were not recorded in this book. Writing this book has given me a greater desire to learn more and discover more hidden treasures in His Word.

About The Author

Dr. Rick Kurnow

Rick was raised in a Jewish home. At age 17 a Japanese friend pointed Him to his Messiah Yeshua (Jesus). Ricks life was radically changed when he invited Yeshua into his life. That was in 1974. He immediately knew he had a call on his life and entered Bethany Bible College in Santa Cruz, California. He received a Bachelor of Science degree as a ministerial major. Rick met his wife Dottie at Bible College and they were married in 1978. Together they have ministered in churches and traveled for over 35 years. Rick has been mightily used of God to impact many lives. The gifts of the Holy Spirit flow richly through his ministry. In 2005 Rick received a Doctor of Divinity from The School of Bible Theology Seminary and University in San Jacinto, California, Dr. Kurnow currently an Associate Pastor along with with his wife Dottie, At Theophany Ministries International under the leadership of Apostle Al Forniss. Also Rick and Dottie frequently speak and minister throughout the USA and Mexico through Kurnow Ministries International. You can find out more about their ministry at *www.Kurnow.org*

Dr's Rick & Dottie Kurnow

Rick is also a recording artist with the release of 3 music CD's recorded with his wife Dottie. His most recent CD is "Here Comes a Miracle." He is also the designer of the New Covenant Messianic Tallit Prayer Shawl. Thousands of these prayer shawls have touched lives all over the world. Dr. Kurnow's DVD teachings "The Biblical use of the Shofar", "The Biblical Use of The Tallit" and "Yeshua Revealed in the Passover" have been distributed all over the world and have been a blessing to many.

Rick & Dottie are the founders of Shofars From Afar, LLC a company that supports the economy of Israel by offering Jewish, Messianic and Christian products. These unique gifts can be found at _www.ShofarsFromAfar.com_

Other books are available by Dr. Kurnow:

Supernatural Is Natural – The Blessings of Hearing The Voice of God
(Also available in Spanish)

Supernatural Is Natural – Miracles, Signs and Wonders
(Also available in Spanish)

Prophetic Words For Daily Living

Learning to Love God's Way

These books and more can be found at:

www.ShofarsFromAFar.com

Made in the USA
San Bernardino, CA
11 March 2017